For my family

Many thanks to Jill Norman, Jim Bunker,
Mark Lucas, Margaret Asher, Jane Scougal and Paul and Jane Kemp
for all their hard work and support.
A special thank you to Gerald, Katy, Alexander and Rory.

All the ready-to-use icing and most of the
ready-made decorations used in the book are made by Supercook
and can be found in all good supermarkets.
I also used some of the wonderful range of decorations
made by Mary Ford Cake Artistry Centre Ltd,
28 Southbourne Grove, Bournemouth BH6 3RA.

This edition published 1986 by Book Club Associates
by arrangement with Walker Books Ltd
First published 1986 by Walker Books Ltd

© 1986 Myriad Productions Ltd
Photographs by Paul Kemp
Illustrations by John Woodcock

First printed 1986
Printed and bound in Italy by L.E.G.O., Vicenza

JANE ASHER'S
Quick Party Cakes

ONLY
7923
CALORIES...

GUILD PUBLISHING
LONDON

CONTENTS

Ready-made cakes, chocolates, marzipan, jellies, biscuits, sweets, icing sugar and decorations—a selection of ingredients that can be quickly transformed into glorious, imaginative cakes that will delight family and friends

INTRODUCTION

I have always enjoyed decorating cakes and I used to spend hours making very ornate and complicated designs for my family and friends, and particularly for our young daughter. In the last few years however two extremely boisterous and time consuming boys have crashed into our lives and I find that now we have three children my cake-decorating ambitions have had to endure heavy cutbacks. I sometimes feel I'll be lucky to find time to stick a candle in a doughnut for some imminent celebration.

Naturally the children still expect special cakes on birthdays and other occasions and I'm now usually given my order some time in advance. Alexander, the 4 year old, in particular seems to think I'm capable of producing the impossible – he's quite likely to request the whole of the A-Team doing battle with Masters of the Universe, with Superman and Spiderman looking on.

It does mean I have had to find a lot of short cuts and easy ways of achieving an effect, and there are such good ready-made cakes and decorations in the supermarket that it has not been too difficult. Few of the cakes in this book will take more than an hour to put together, some of them considerably less and none of them is very difficult.

If you have time though, of course homemade cakes and icing will taste better and be cheaper, so I have given basic recipes for these. Do keep looking out in the shops for interestingly shaped ingredients that may inspire you to produce a new idea.

Now that we are all aware of the devastat-

ing effect of sugar on children's teeth, I try to limit sweet things in our house and only make iced cakes for very special occasions. I hope that you enjoy this book of party cakes and that when that special occasion does arrive, the speed of the designs will give you less time in the kitchen and more time to relax and enjoy the results.

9

CAT & KITTENS

1 large sponge flan case / 1 tube ready-to-use chocolate icing
½ lb/250 g fondant icing or marzipan
red, green and blue colouring / 1 chocolate Swiss roll
small quantity of white icing / chocolate drops
chocolate buttons / 1 liquorice whirl / 1 chocolate finger biscuit
6 chocolate mini rolls / gold balls / Matchmakers

If this is done for a child's birthday you could make a suitable number of kittens and give each one a candle for a tail, and the flan could be piped with basketwork icing if you have time.
The poor cat looks a bit fed up, but any mother might be at having to share a bed with all those offspring!

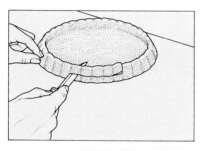

1 Cut a piece off the edge of the flan to make the front of the basket. Spread the flan with chocolate icing.

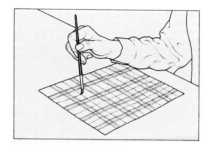

2 Roll out the fondant or marzipan and cut a square. Paint tartan stripes on it, then drape it onto the flan case. Snip two edges to make fringes.

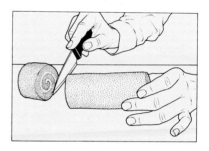

3 Cut a generous quarter off the large Swiss roll. Cover raw ends with chocolate icing.

6 Make the kittens in the same way with mini rolls, using gold balls for eyes, Matchmakers for tails and quarter chocolate buttons for ears. Place cat and kittens in basket.

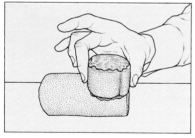

4 Turn small piece and stick to large piece with icing to form mother cat's head.

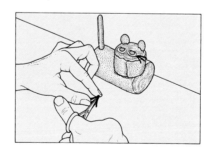

5 Put blobs of white icing and chocolate drops for eyes and half chocolate buttons for ears. Unroll liquorice and cut off 2 in/ 5 cm lengths. Snip into whiskers and stick to face. Add chocolate finger for tail.

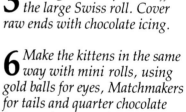

CARS

1 block Madeira cake / 2 trifle sponges
1 tube ready-to-use red icing
1 tube ready-to-use blue icing
4 chocolate mini rolls / rice paper
1 liquorice whirl / jellies / mints
edible decorating pen

Cars are always popular for birthday cakes and this version is very simple to do. You don't have to crash them, of course, but it does make quite a dramatic centrepiece and clearly in this pile-up no one was hurt.

1 *Trim cake straight at edges then slice in half lengthways.*

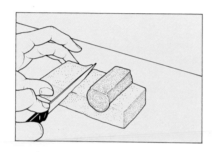

2 *Scoop two half circles out of each for wheels to fit into.*

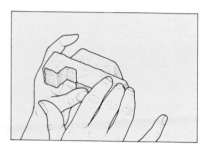

3 *Stick a trifle sponge to the top of each one and cover one with red and one with blue icing. Smooth with wet fingers. Let dry.*

4 *Put cars on mini roll wheels. Cut window shapes out of rice paper and stick in position with tiny quantity of icing.*

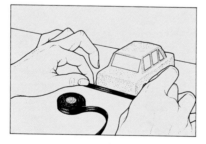

5 *Undo liquorice whirl and cut strips for bumpers. Stick to fronts and backs.*

6 *Stick yellow jellies for lights and mints for hub caps. Cut rice paper number plates and write suitable message. Stick to fronts and backs.*

KNITTING

This is such fun to do and is easier than you might think. It would be lovely for a grandmother's birthday or for any other keen knitter, and you could always pipe some fancier stitches or use different coloured icing.

2 packets sponge mix
1 tube ready-to-use pink icing
1 round doughnut
4 long Matchmakers
2 chocolate drops

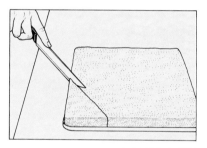

1 *Bake sponge in a shallow rectangular baking tray. When cool, neaten the edges and cut corner off one end.*

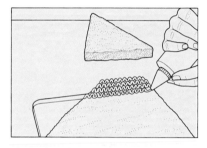

2 *Spread all over with some of the icing. With small round nozzle, pipe wavy lines of plain knitting from top to bottom.*

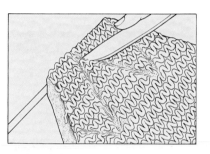

3 *With knife, mark folds of knitting at the top.*

6 *Melt one end of a Matchmaker and stick on a chocolate drop. When set lay it across the top end of knitting and pipe stitches over it. Make other needle in similar way and push into ball of wool. Stick two more Matchmakers into other side to look like ends of needles. Put ball of wool in position.*

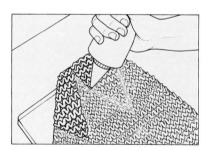

4 *Pipe extra knitting on to each fold to create bunched up effect.*

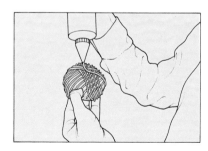

5 *Cover doughnut with icing then pipe strands of wool across it.*

CHICKEN POX

1 round jam sponge
1 tube ready-to-use white icing
1 tube ready-to-use chocolate icing
red and blue Smarties
candle
felt tip pen

Children don't normally feel ill for very long with chicken pox so this could be a nice cake to cheer them up and make them laugh when they're on the mend. Our two boys got it at the same time recently and looked almost as spotty as this.

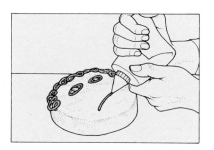

1 *Spread top and side of sponge with white icing.*

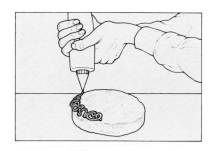

2 *Pipe curly hair with chocolate icing.*

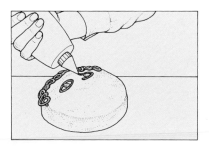

3 *Press in Smartie eyes and pipe around with chocolate.*

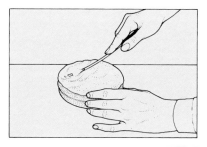

4 *Pipe chocolate nose and mouth.*

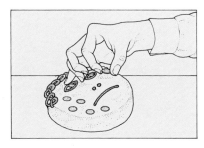

5 *Press in red Smartie spots.*

6 *Mark candle as thermometer with felt tip and push into mouth.*

PARCEL

1 block sponge (2 packets sponge mix baked in loaf tin)
1½ lb/750 g fondant
jam
green and red colouring
1 black edible decorating pen
1 egg white

Fondant looks very like paper when used in this way, and you could wrap any shape of cake and use it for various special occasions.

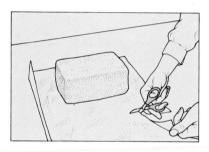

1 *Cut a piece of paper big enough to wrap around most of cake.*

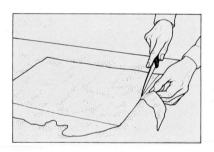

2 *Roll out fondant, place paper on top as guide and cut round edge. Wrap scraps of fondant in plastic or foil.*

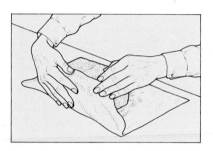

3 *Brush cake with jam. Wrap fondant around cake making real envelope ends and leaving one side mostly uncovered.*

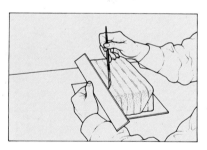

4 *Turn bare side underneath. Paint suitable wrapping paper design with brush and colourings.*

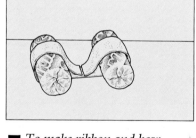

5 *To make ribbon and bow colour most of remaining fondant by kneading in a few drops of colouring. Roll out and cut a long strip. Fold ends over suitable round shapes and stick with a little water in the middle. Leave to dry.*

6 *Cut two long strips to wrap around parcel. Moisten and stick on. Stick bow carefully to centre of parcel. Cut two short strips for bow ends, stick to bow. Cover with further small piece of fondant. Cut label with pinking shears. When dry write message with edible pen and stick on parcel. Glaze ribbon with a little egg white.*

Happy Birthday to Margaret
Love from Jane
xx

CLOWN

It does take a little time to cover him with icing but I think this happy clown is worth the effort and would brighten up any party if he sat on the table.

1 firm round Madeira cake / 1½ lb/750 g fondant / jam
3 jam mini rolls / ¼ packet chocolate cake covering
1 round doughnut / rice paper / 1 tube ready-to-use red icing
1 glacé cherry / 1 tube ready-to-use blue icing
round liquorice allsorts – large and small
1 ice cream cone / 2 ready-to-use icing hands

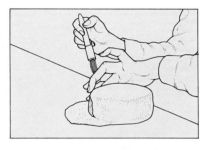

1 *Roll out 1 lb/500 g of the fondant. Spread the cake with jam and then cover with the fondant.*

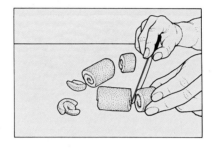

2 *Cut a third from 2 of the mini rolls. Trim ends of larger pieces at an angle to fit onto body.*

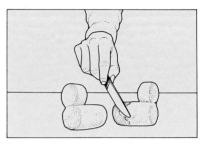

3 *Stick small pieces on top of large pieces to form shoes. Roll out remaining fondant. Cover feet and legs. Melt chocolate and pour carefully over feet. Let dry.*

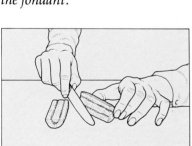

4 *Stick legs to body with a little icing. Cut last mini roll in half lengthwise and cover both halves with fondant.*

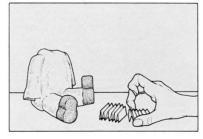

5 *Cover doughnut with fondant. Stick arms in place. Pleat a large strip of rice paper and cut in half lengthwise. Fan out and stick in circle for ruff. Stick doughnut on top.*

6 *Pipe curly red hair. Stick cherry nose with icing or melted chocolate. Pipe red mouth and blue eyes. Stick pom poms onto body, shoes and cone. Stick cone to head, and hands onto sleeves.*

CASTLE

1 large square sponge (3 packets sponge mix)
2–3 packets plain chocolate cake covering
3 packets miniature Milky Way or Marathon
2 Swiss rolls / 4 flat rectangular chocolate mints
3 chocolate finger biscuits
1 tube ready-to-use white icing
1 tube ready-to-use blue icing
6 Matchmakers / rice paper / edible decorating pen

Alexander, my 4 year old, very kindly insisted on lending me one of his precious soldiers when I told him I was making a castle, which explains the slightly surprising presence of the English Tommy in this medieval scene. This would be a good cake for a large children's party.

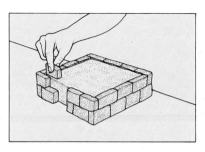

1 *Trim cake to an even square or rectangle. With melted chocolate cake covering stick two rows of Milky Way 'bricks' around base, leaving a small gap on one side.*

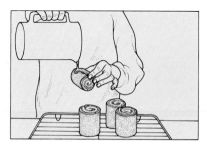

2 *Cut both Swiss rolls in half then cover with melted chocolate. Leave a few minutes to dry.*

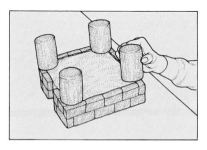

3 *Stick a Swiss roll turret to each corner with a little more melted chocolate then build up another row of bricks between. Stick half bricks on top for castellations.*

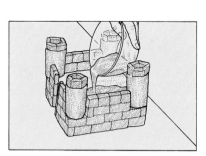

4 *Pour melted chocolate onto top of sponge. Spread evenly and leave to set.*

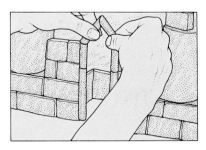

5 *Cut away a piece of sponge inside gateway. Cover the cut edges with 3 mints. Make an arch with chocolate fingers.*

6 *Pipe white icing between bricks with small nozzle. Ice a blue moat onto board and place a mint and Matchmaker drawbridge. Cut rice paper flags and decorate with edible pen. Stick to Matchmakers with a little chocolate. Make holes in turrets with a skewer and place a flag in each.*

CLOWN

It does take a little time to cover him with icing but I think this happy clown is worth the effort and would brighten up any party if he sat on the table.

1 firm round Madeira cake / 1½ lb / 750 g fondant / jam
3 jam mini rolls / ¼ packet chocolate cake covering
1 round doughnut / rice paper / 1 tube ready-to-use red icing
1 glacé cherry / 1 tube ready-to-use blue icing
round liquorice allsorts – large and small
1 ice cream cone / 2 ready-to-use icing hands

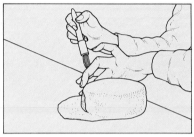

1 *Roll out 1 lb/500 g of the fondant. Spread the cake with jam and then cover with the fondant.*

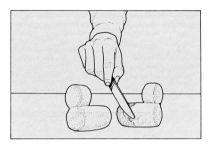

2 *Cut a third from 2 of the mini rolls. Trim ends of larger pieces at an angle to fit onto body.*

3 *Stick small pieces on top of large pieces to form shoes. Roll out remaining fondant. Cover feet and legs. Melt chocolate and pour carefully over feet. Let dry.*

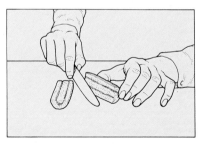

4 *Stick legs to body with a little icing. Cut last mini roll in half lengthwise and cover both halves with fondant.*

5 *Cover doughnut with fondant. Stick arms in place. Pleat a large strip of rice paper and cut in half lengthwise. Fan out and stick in circle for ruff. Stick doughnut on top.*

6 *Pipe curly red hair. Stick cherry nose with icing or melted chocolate. Pipe red mouth and blue eyes. Stick pom poms onto body, shoes and cone. Stick cone to head, and hands onto sleeves.*

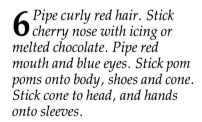

VASE

1 plain Swiss roll
½ lb/250 g fondant / jam
edible wafer flowers and leaves
long angelica / chocolate cake covering
1 tube ready-to-use green icing
1 tube ready-to-use blue icing

It can be hard to find long angelica but some large stores do have it. If you can't get hold of it then long Matchmakers look almost as good.

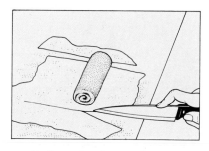

1 *Roll out fondant, trim edges and cut slightly wider than the Swiss roll.*

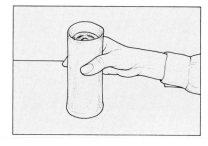

2 *Spread the cake with jam and roll it up in the fondant, letting the extra width stick up at the top.*

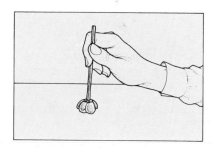

3 *Stick wafer rose onto angelica stems by using melted chocolate and holding in place for a few seconds until set. Squeeze little green icing leaves over the join.*

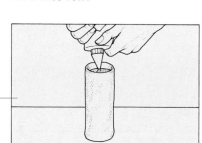

4 *Squeeze a little blue icing into the top of the vase.*

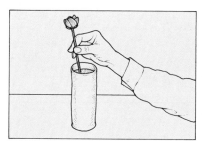

5 *Push the flowers gently into the vase.*

6 *Put the cake in position. Carefully stick on the wafer leaves with a little icing or melted chocolate.*

HUMPTY DUMPTY

1–2 packets miniature Milky Way or Marathon
1 tube ready-to-use white icing / 1 round jam sponge
1 tube ready-to-use red icing
1 tube ready-to-use blue icing
two trifle sponge fingers / chocolate buttons

When I had just made this and had it ready to be photographed Humpty really did quite suddenly fall off and crash onto the table. It was annoying at the time but seems quite funny when I look back on it – almost as if he had to fulfil his destiny . . .

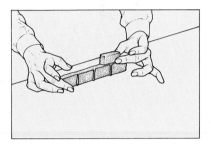

1 *Build wall up with at least two thicknesses of Milky Way 'bricks', sticking them together with white icing.*

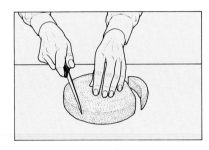

2 *Trim sponge cake to a more egg-like shape.*

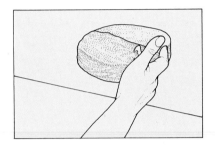

3 *Spread lower half of cake with red icing, smoothing with wet fingers.*

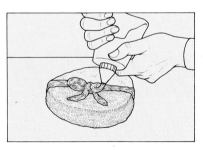

4 *Spread upper half with white icing, and again smooth with wet fingers. Using shell nozzle pipe belt and bow in blue to cover join.*

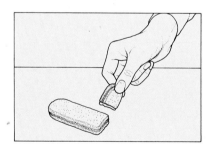

5 *Cut a quarter off trifle sponge fingers. Turn and stick upright with a little icing to form feet.*

6 *Stick Humpty carefully onto wall with icing. Pipe blue eyes and add chocolate drop pupils, and a red mouth. Stick legs onto wall.*
For crashed Humpty make egg with half peach and whipped cream.

26

DESK

This makes a very large cake and would be suitable for an office party or celebration of promotion. The photograph makes it nicely personal and you can write something suitable for the occasion on the rice paper letter.

6 slabs of Madeira cake
1 large rectangular sponge (3 packets sponge mix)
3–4 packets plain chocolate cake covering
1 tube ready-to-use chocolate icing
candied lemons / 3 chocolate mini rolls / mint crisps / rice paper
angelica / edible decorating pen / wafer roses / Matchmakers
tiny amount of white fondant and blue icing / photograph

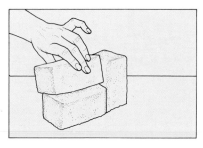

1 *Trim packet cakes and stick together in threes to make two drawer units.*

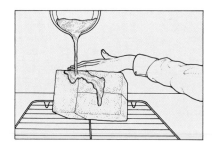

2 *Stand on grid and cover with melted chocolate, catching excess to use again.*

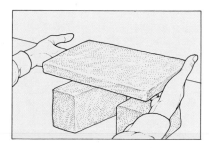

3 *Try top for size and trim as necessary. Cover with chocolate and stick onto the drawer units.*

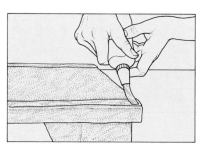

4 *With leaf tube pipe flat edges to desk top.*

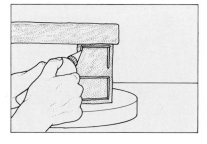

5 *With small nozzle pipe drawer fronts. Stick trimmed lemons onto drawers for handles.*

6 *Make fittings for desk top as desired. Vase as page 24, using mini roll, blotter from rice paper and mint crisps, pencil holder and bin from mini rolls. Calendar and photo frame from mint crisps and icing.*

PRETTY LADY

1 small doll
1 pudding basin sponge (2 packets sponge mix)
white icing
1 lb/500 g fondant
silver balls
1 round ring biscuit
sugar flowers

You can, of course, buy china figures made especially for these sort of cakes, but I think using a real doll looks much nicer and less old fashioned. The draped fondant is very quick and makes an elegant skirt.

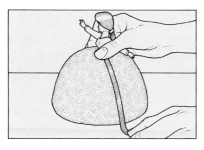

1 *Make hole in top of cake and try doll for size. Measure from centre of hole to hem of skirt with string. Remove doll.*

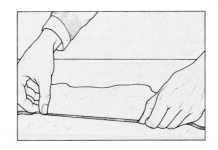

2 *Spread cake with icing. Roll out fondant and using string as radius measure a circle.*

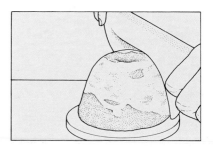

3 *Cut out circle. Roll onto rolling pin and pick up. Unroll onto cake.*

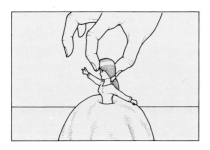

4 *Push doll gently through icing into cake. Pipe icing around waist and add silver balls.*

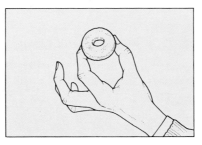

5 *Spread icing over biscuit and add flowers and silver balls.*

6 *Stick hat to head, pipe decorations onto skirt and add flowers and silver balls. Stick flowers on shoulders.*

CRADLE

This would make a lovely christening cake and the parents could keep the baby doll as a reminder of a happy day. It could also be used as a first birthday cake.

1 round chocolate covered sponge
¼ lb/125 g fondant
½ packet plain chocolate cake covering
thin crisp rectangular chocolate mints
blue or pink decorating gel
1 tiny baby doll

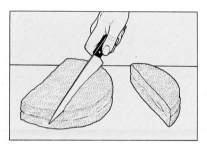

1 *Cut cake into three.*

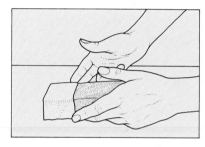

2 *Roll out fondant. Cut a small strip, moisten slightly and stick over end of centre section of sponge.*

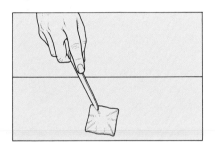

3 *Cut a thicker piece to be the pillow – mark creases with the back of a knife. Put pillow in position and put baby on pillow.*

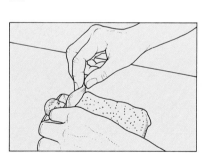

4 *Roll and cut piece of fondant and mark with a fork to look like baby blanket. Moisten blanket and stick onto cradle. Tuck a small strip of fondant under pillow end and fold over edge of blanket for top sheet.*

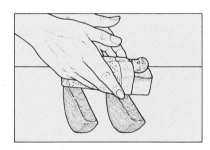

5 *Spread 'raw' sides of rockers with melted chocolate and position cradle on them. Leave a few minutes to stick.*

6 *Spread sides and end of cradle with melted chocolate and cover with mint crisps, trimming to fit as necessary. Stick headboard crisps upright. Decorate blanket with suitable coloured gel.*

ROCKET

½ lb/250 g fondant
1 Swiss roll
jam
edible red decorating pen
2 ice cream wafers
1 packet Rolos
1 coloured ice cream cone

Don't worry if you can't find the coloured ice cream cone – a plain one would do. You could make an effective moon surface with rock cake mix and brown sugar if you want to put the rocket in a setting.

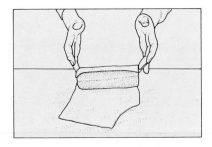

1 *Roll out fondant and cut to width of Swiss roll. Spread cake with jam and cover with fondant.*

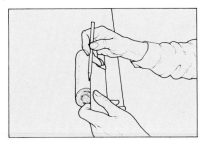

2 *Decorate side of rocket with edible pen.*

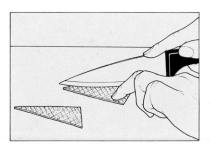

3 *Cut 2 wafers diagonally with sharp knife.*

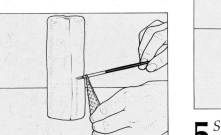

4 *Stick 3 wings onto rocket by moistening the fondant and pressing them in.*

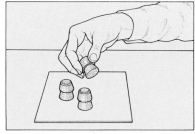

5 *Stick 3 lots of Rolos together with jam to make boosters.*

6 *Stick cone to top of rocket. Brush jam on top of boosters then stand rocket on top of them.*

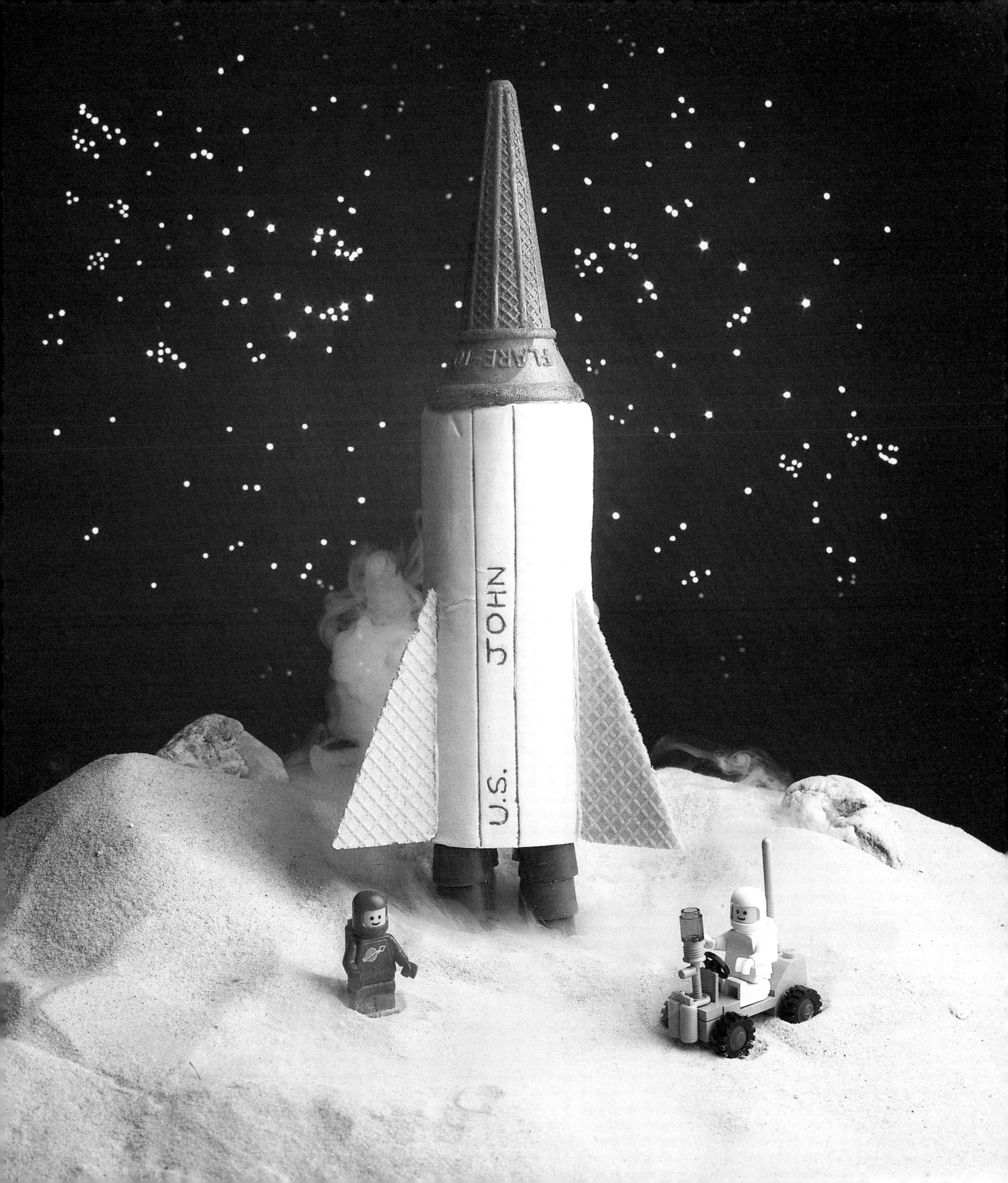
U.S.
JOHN

SAMPLER

1 large shallow rectangular sponge (2 packets sponge mix)
¾ lb/375 g fondant
jam
5 long packets of Toblerone
chocolate cake covering
Matchmakers
ready-made icing letters and roses as necessary

You can find packets of ready-made letters in supermarkets and combined with the chocolate frame they make a lovely old fashioned sampler. You may have to buy several packets to be able to make your chosen message, but any spare letters will keep and may be useful later.

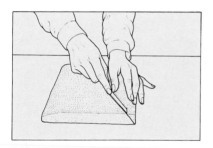

1 *Trim edges of cake to make sloping sides.*

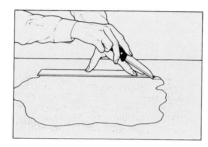

2 *Measure top of cake excluding sloping edges. Roll out fondant and cut to fit.*

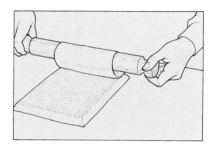

3 *Spread cake lightly with jam. Pick up fondant on rolling pin and transfer onto top of cake.*

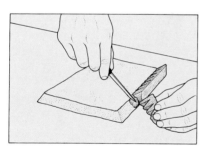

4 *With melted chocolate stick Toblerone frame around edges, joining as necessary, and holding for a few seconds to set.*

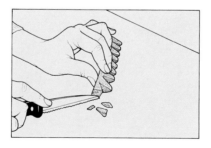

5 *Mitre the corners by cutting Toblerone at an angle with very sharp or serrated knife.*

6 *Fill in cracks at corner with pieces of Matchmaker. Try out message and flowers until satisfied and then stick in place with tiny blobs of fondant mixed in water.*

LOCH NESS MONSTER

1 chocolate mini roll / 3 pieces Toblerone
chocolate cake covering / 1 tube ready-to-use white icing
2 chocolate drops / 2 Matchmakers
1 tube ready-to-use blue icing / 1 tube ready-to-use green icing
1 rectangular sponge (2 packets sponge mix baked in baking
tray) / 2 chocolate whirls

There's no doubt our Nessie is very much real and has surfaced from the deep. Any round cakes or biscuits would give the same effect – even doughnuts – but you would need to cover them with icing or melted chocolate to match the head.

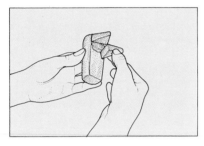

1 *Stick 2 pieces of Toblerone to mini roll with melted chocolate or a little icing to form Nessie's head.*

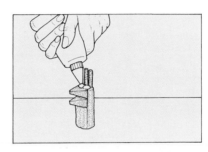

2 *Pipe white eyes and teeth, add chocolate drop pupils and push in Matchmaker antennae.*

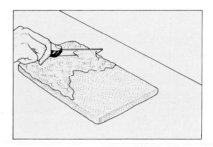

3 *Spread mixed green and blue icing over cake with knife, lifting it into little waves.*

6 *Add a piece of Toblerone behind body to make tail.*

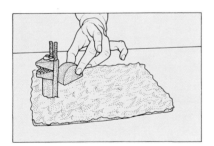

4 *Push head into icing. Cut whirls in uneven pieces and place in decreasing size behind head to form body.*

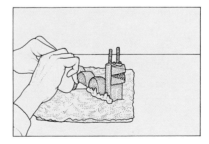

5 *Pipe white surf with shell nozzle around monster.*

NEST

1 sponge cake with hole in the middle (2 packets sponge mix baked in ring mould)
1 tube ready-to-use chocolate icing
¼ lb / 125 g fondant
hard boiled egg / fluffy chickens

All sorts of little gifts could go inside the egg shells of this cake if not to be used for Easter. You could even put a little money in them for a very special birthday and make it a real nest-egg!

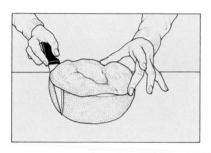

1 *Trim cake so that it will stand straight.*

2 *Put spare bits of cake into centre. Spread sides, top and inside with chocolate icing then mark with a fork.*

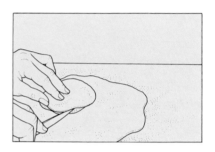

3 *Roll out fondant. Cut a circle large enough to cover three quarters of the egg, flouring it well first.*

6 *Put little chicks in nest and cover with shells.*

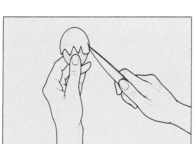

4 *Cut broken jagged edges around fondant. Leave to dry standing in egg box or similar.*

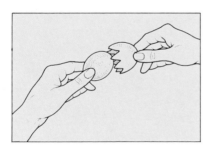

5 *When set hard remove carefully from egg. Make 3 more in same way.*

FAIRY CASTLE

With the fruit inside and cream spread between the cake and meringue this makes a delicious pudding, and if you use the ready-made meringues it's very quick to do.

1 kugelhopf or ring cake
double cream or white icing
1 box of party meringues
silver balls / rosebud sugar flowers
fresh or tinned fruit
1 meringue flan / 1 tiny fairy

1 *Put cake onto a suitable board or plate. If using cream, whip till thick, then spread it or icing around bottom of cake. Stick meringues around leaving a gap for entrance.*

2 *Stick second row in the same way then cut an archway through to the centre.*

3 *Pipe icing or cream around archway and decorate with silver balls and rosebuds.*

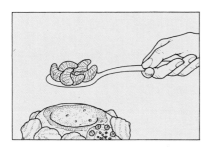

4 *Pile fruit into centre of ring if desired.*

5 *Stick silver balls with icing or cream to point of each meringue.*

6 *Stick meringue flan to top of ring. Stick three meringues in centre to form spire. Decorate with roses and silver balls. Stick fairy in entrance.*

DACHSHUND

1 chocolate sponge Swiss roll
chocolate cake covering / 2 chocolate mini rolls
liquorice stick / 1 rum truffle cake
rice paper / liquorice whirl
1 tube ready-to-use red icing
silver balls

More of a Swiss roll dog than a sausage dog but he looks quite friendly. By cutting pieces of cake to shape you could make more or less any breed of dog as a birthday cake for its owner – as long as they don't expect an exact likeness.

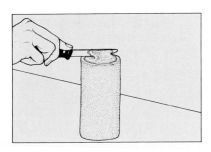

1 *Spread melted cake covering over ends of Swiss roll.*

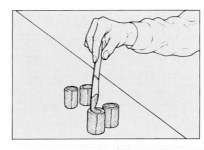

2 *Cut mini rolls in half, put into position and spread tops with chocolate.*

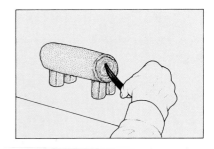

3 *Put body onto legs. Cut liquorice stick to a point with sharp scissors for tail then stick with more chocolate into one end of cake.*

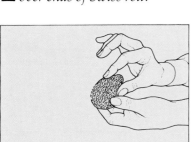

4 *Mould truffle into muzzle shape with fingers.*

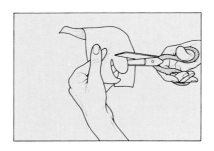

5 *Cut ear shapes out of rice paper. Spread ears with chocolate and stick to head.*

6 *Stick on scraps of liquorice for eyes and nose. Stick head to body. Make a collar with red icing and silver balls. Add a lead of unwound liquorice whirl.*

44

SHIP

Some cake mixes have rice paper faces included in the pack and I thought they would make effective portholes. You may also find the faces on their own with the cake decorations in the local supermarket, but if you can't get either, just cut some out of rice paper and decorate them.

1 large rectangular sponge (2 packets sponge mix)
1 lb/500 g fondant / jam
3 trifle sponges / 1 tube ready-to-use chocolate icing
2 chocolate mini rolls
1 tube ready-to-use blue icing / rice paper faces
iced ring biscuit
ready-to-use red icing for lifebelt

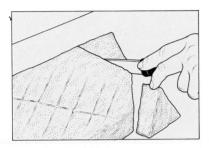

1 Cut corners off one end of cake to make prow.

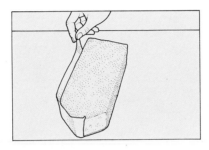

2 Roll out fondant and cut pieces to cover boat neatly, allowing ½ in/1 cm extra height round deck. Stick with jam.

3 Wrap the trifle sponges with fondant, after spreading with jam, to make cabin.

6 Stick cartoon faces onto sides of ship and pipe round portholes with chocolate icing. Spread blue icing onto cake board. Ice ring biscuit to look like life belt and attach to ship with icing 'rope'.

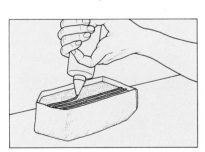

4 Pipe chocolate lines along deck and then position cabin on deck.

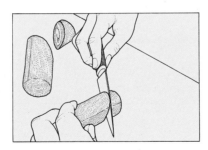

5 Cut ends off mini rolls at an angle then stick to top of cabin with chocolate icing.

FRIED EGGS ON TOAST

This must be one of the quickest cakes in the book if you use a ready-made sponge and an aerosol of cream – it's very silly, but, I think, enormous fun.

1 rectangular flat sponge
tin of half peaches
whipped cream or aerosol cream

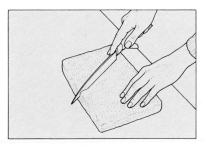

1 *Cut sponge in half to look like two pieces of toast.*

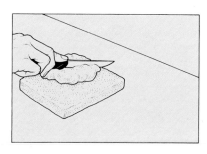

2 *Spread or spray cream onto sponge cakes.*

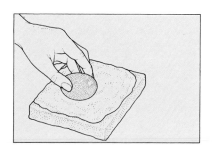

3 *Press peach halves into cream.*

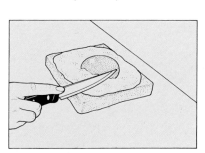

4 *Pull cream up around peaches with a knife.*

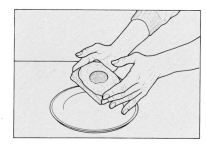

5 *Put on a plate.*

6 *Add a knife and fork if desired for fun.*

TRAIN

There are lots of ways of making a train but this is wonderfully easy and I'm pleased with the way the mini rolls raise it up as if on real wheels. You could make the track go right down the centre of the table for a large party.

For train and 4 trucks:
3 large chocolate Swiss rolls
1 packet chocolate cake covering
11 chocolate mini rolls
sweets / 1 packet Rolos
For track: 2 liquorice whirls
1 packet long Matchmakers / chopped nuts

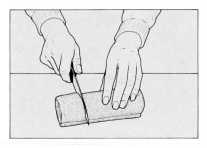

1 *Cut a third off one Swiss roll.*

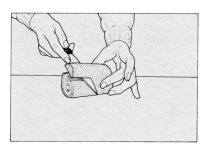

4 *For trucks cut other Swiss rolls in half. Slice top off each half. Spread trucks with melted chocolate and press sweets into them.*

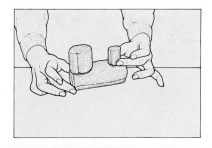

2 *Turn the smaller piece and stick on top of larger one with melted cake covering. Cut one mini roll in half and stick one to other end.*

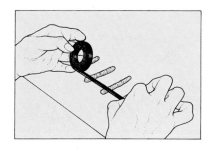

5 *Make track with Matchmakers and unwound liquorice, finally sprinkling nuts in between.*

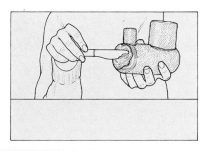

3 *Cover ends of Swiss roll with melted chocolate.*

6 *Stick two mini rolls with melted chocolate under engine and each truck for wheels. Stick a Rolo on top of engine and two on front for buffers. Add two buffers to back of last truck. Place engine and trucks carefully onto the track.*

STAG NIGHT

This doll is the same type that I used for the Fairy Ring – from innocent fairy to voluptuous showgirl with just a little added icing!

one 8 in/20 cm round fruit cake
one 6 in/15 cm round fruit cake
1½ lb/750 g fondant icing/jam
1 tube ready-to-use white icing
1 tube ready-to-use pink icing
2 tiny pink balls
doll

1 *Cut a strip of fondant to cover sides of smaller cake. Spread cake with jam and roll onto fondant.*

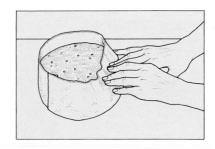

2 *Cut a strip for larger cake deep enough to cover sides and half of the top. Stick fondant on with jam.*

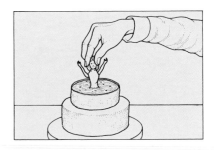

3 *Stick cakes together by wetting the icing. Make a hole through both and try doll in it to get the size right. Remove.*

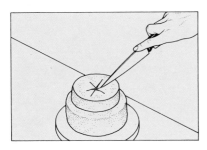

4 *Spread outer ring of top of cake with jam and cover entire top with fondant. Cut slashes away from centre with a sharp knife.*

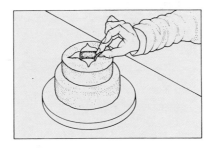

5 *Pull up 'torn' pieces from the centre of the cake. Brush off crumbs as necessary.*

6 *Pipe pink breasts onto the doll and put on pink nipples. Push her into the cake. Pipe traditional icing around the edges of cake.*

POND

1 large sponge flan case
1 tube ready-to-use blue icing
1 tube ready-to-use green icing
icing flowers
candle holders / china frogs
chopped nuts

My daughter collects china frogs and I made this cake for her birthday a few years ago. For the book she lent me some frogs from her collection – you could also use little marzipan ones.

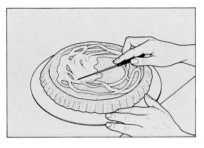

1 *Spread base of flan case with blue icing.*

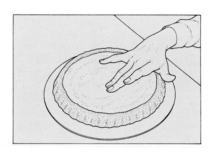

2 *Smooth with wet fingers.*

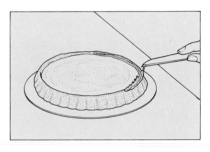

3 *Spread green icing around edges then lift with knife to look like grass.*

6 *Arrange a chopped nut path around pond and add little frogs as desired.*

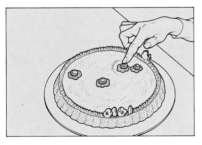

4 *Press candle holders into pond for lilies, stick flowers into grass.*

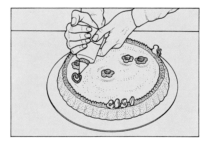

5 *Ice green leaves around lilies.*

DIET CAKE

2 ready-made large sponge flan cases
1 pint/600 ml whipped cream
selection of cakes, chocolates, sweets etc
paper tape measure
rice paper
edible decorating pen
angelica or Matchmaker
ice cream wafer

Well if you can't break your diet on your birthday when can you? And if you're going to break it then you might as well go right over the top and be thoroughly wicked. For women who worry a little too much about their figure it might even do them good to have a laugh about it.

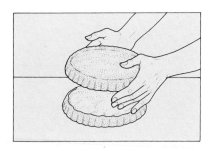

1 *Sandwich flans together with whipped cream. Put on cake dish.*

2 *Layer cream and goodies onto sponge.*

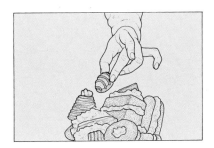

3 *Pile up as high as you possibly can!*

4 *Stick the tape measure round the cake and trim as necessary.*

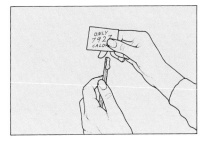

5 *Cut a piece of rice paper and write the calorie count with edible pen. Stick to the angelica with a little cream.*

6 *Push the label into the top of the cake. Fill in any gaps with cream, perch the wafer on the top.*

ONLY
7923
CALORIES....

FITNESS CAKE

1 deep round sponge (2 packets sponge mix)
jam
½ lb/250 g fondant icing
1 tube ready-to-use pink icing
pink Smarties
edible decorating pen
4 chocolate whirls
2 chocolate mini rolls

After the diet cake how about a little jog to lose those extra pounds? So many people have got caught up in the exercise craze that this could be a very popular cake. Or perhaps a sportsclub could use it as a centrepiece at a party.

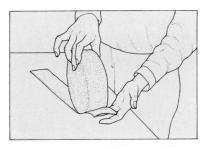

1 *Spread cake with jam. Roll out fondant thinly and use to cover sides and top.*

2 *With shell nozzle pipe pink shell pattern around top and bottom edges.*

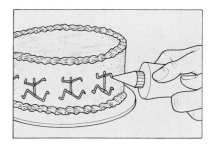

3 *With small nozzle pipe running figures around side.*

6 *Position dumb-bells on top of cake. Run round the block before and after eating!*

4 *Stick smarties on for heads and draw faces with decorating pen.*

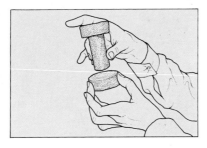

5 *With a little icing stick a chocolate whirl to each end of the mini roll.*

CRACKERS

1 lb/500 g fondant
colouring
1 Swiss roll
jam
edible flowers and leaves

Yet another use for the Swiss roll – simple and quick to make and very effective. A small one at each place for the Christmas table would look beautiful, or even several of them in a fondant box as a centrepiece.

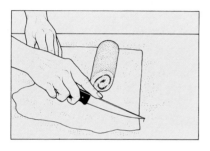

1 *Put aside a small amount of the white fondant and colour the rest by kneading in a few drops of colouring. Roll out fondant about half as wide again as Swiss roll. Trim edges.*

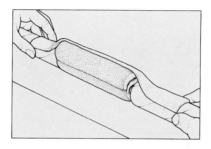

2 *Spread cake with jam. Place a well-floured cardboard tube (such as inside of roll of foil or clingfilm) each end of cake and roll up in fondant. Moisten the edge of the fondant to join firmly.*

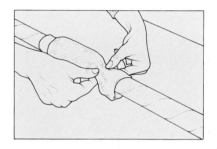

3 *Squeeze gathers between cake and tubes to make cracker shape. Leave to dry.*

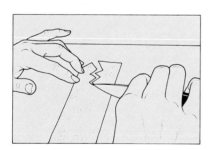

4 *Roll out strip of white fondant. Cut zigzag down centre.*

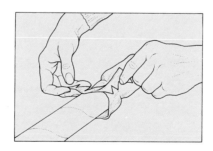

5 *Stick a strip to each end of cracker.*

6 *Decorate with edible flowers and leaves. When hard very gently remove tubes. Make small crackers in the same way with mini rolls and small tubes (Smarties or similar).*

ROBOT

2 slab fruit cakes / jam
2–3 packets white marzipan / 4 chocolate whirls
1 tube ready-to-use white icing
1 trifle sponge / liquorice whirl / sweets / silver balls
1 glacé cherry / 2 Matchmakers

I wonder if we ever will be using robots to work for us in the home – I'd be quite happy for this little chap to come along and do my washing up.

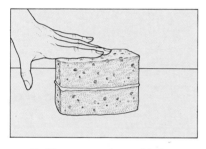

1 *Roll out marzipan thinly. Stick cakes together with jam and marzipan.*

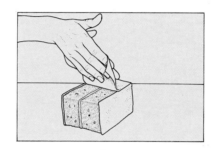

2 *Spread with jam and cover with marzipan.*

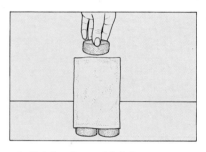

3 *Stick cakes with icing onto two chocolate whirls for feet. Stick another on top for neck.*

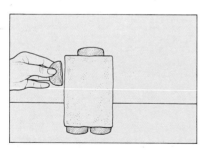

4 *Cut the last whirl in half and stick with icing to each side for arms.*

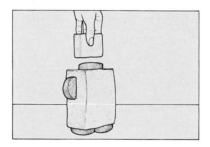

5 *Wrap the trifle sponge in marzipan and stick onto neck for head.*

6 *Decorate with sweets. Pipe icing along edges and cover with silver balls. Cut cherry in half and stick to head. Add two Matchmaker antennae.*

JAWS

1 large rectangular sponge (3 packets sponge mix baked in baking tin)
1 tube ready-to-use chocolate icing / soft light brown sugar
2 rock cakes / 1 tube ready-to-use blue icing
edible green gel / chocolate shells and prawns / small dolls
Shark: 1 trifle sponge / 1 jaffa cake / white icing / red gel
silver balls / chopped nuts

This is rather gruesome but most of the children I know seem to love a bit of horror! You could leave out the half eaten doll if you want to be slightly more optimistic.

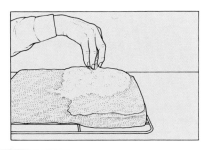

1 *Spread two thirds of cake with chocolate icing. Sprinkle with sugar.*

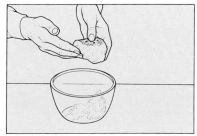

2 *Spread rock cakes with icing and sugar – place on beach.*

3 *Pipe waves onto sand with blue icing then fill in sea on remainder of cake by spreading with knife.*

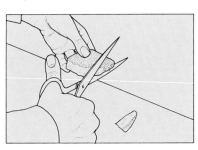

4 *Trim trifle sponge to shape of shark's upper jaw.*

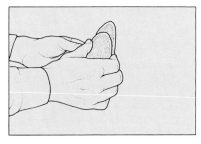

5 *Trim jaffa cake and stick to sponge to make lower jaw.*

6 *Spread red gel inside shark's mouth. Cover outside with white icing. Add eyes (silver balls) and teeth (chopped nuts). Make a hole in sea and insert shark, icing round to make it stick. Add seaweed, shells, dolls and blood!*

WITCH

1 pudding basin sponge (2 packets sponge mix)
1 chocolate mini roll
1 packet chocolate cake covering / 2 chocolate finger biscuits
1 liquorice whirl / 1 rum truffle cake
1 green ice cream cone / 2 long Matchmakers / red decorating gel
chocolate chips / white icing
packet chocolate decorations

It's become a tradition in our house that we have a children's party at Hallowe'en and this witch makes a lovely centrepiece. She doesn't look very sinister – perhaps she's just a learner and can't yet do the really nasty spells.

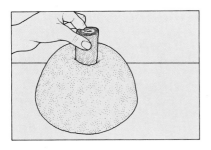

1 *Cut a hole in top of sponge. Trim top of mini roll and push into hole.*

2 *Cover with melted chocolate over grid so that excess can be re-used.*

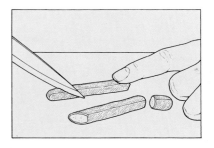

3 *Cut one end straight off finger biscuit and other end off diagonally. Stick to the body with chocolate.*

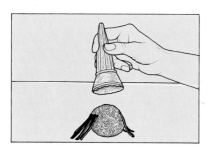

4 *Unravel liquorice and cut strands for hair. Stick to truffle with chocolate and add cone hat.*

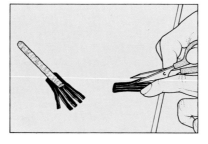

5 *Cut more liquorice and stick to Matchmaker for broom. Stick a liquorice strand around top of bristles.*

6 *Stick broom under arm with chocolate. Pipe hands with red gel. Add eyes with icing and chocolate chips. Use tiny piece of Matchmaker for the nose. Stick head to body. Stick on chocolate decorations.*

ROSE TREES

2 chocolate mini rolls
2 ready-made chocolate dessert cups
1 tube ready-to-use chocolate icing
chocolate strands
2 doughnuts
1 tube ready-to-use green icing
sugar flowers
marzipan leaves

It would be very pretty to make one of these for every place at a tea table or you could put a long avenue of them down the centre.

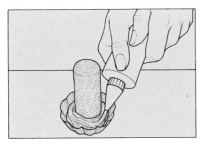

1 *Stand chocolate mini roll in a chocolate cup and fill half way up with chocolate icing.*

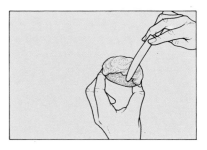

2 *Pour on chocolate strands to look earthy.*

3 *Spread doughnut with green icing.*

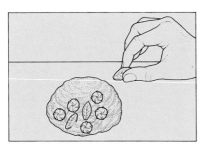

4 *Press sugar flowers and marzipan leaves into icing.*

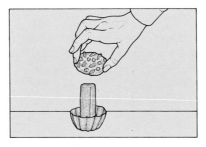

5 *Stick doughnut to mini roll.*

6 *Repeat for second tree. Either make one for each place setting or make a little front door and position one each side as shown.*

CATERPILLAR

1 rum truffle cake
1 tube ready-to-use white icing
chocolate drops
long Matchmakers
1 packet chocolate whirls
Smarties

Another cake that you can adjust easily to the number of children you have to feed – right down the centre of the table or in a wiggly circle it would look very effective.

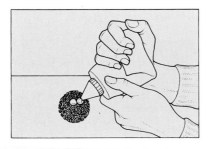

1 *Pipe eyes onto rum truffle with white icing.*

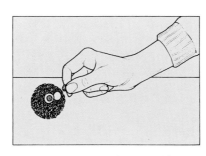

2 *Add chocolate drop pupils.*

3 *Stick Matchmaker antennae into truffle.*

6 *Adjust shape to make desired wiggle.*

4 *Arrange whirls behind head.*

5 *Stick Smarties onto caterpillar with icing.*

COOKER

2 Madeira sponge blocks
approx. 6 sheets rice paper
1 tube ready-to-use white icing
2 wafers / chocolate drops
red decorating gel / liquorice whirls
white sweet for handle
Saucepans: $\frac{1}{4}$ chocolate mini roll / $\frac{1}{2}$ Matchmaker
small quantity of icing / sweets / Smarties etc

Not a very modern cooker – it looks like one my mother used when I was a child – but you just try doing an eye-level grill with icing! And a split level oven would look just like a boring box. You can have great fun with the food in the saucepans.

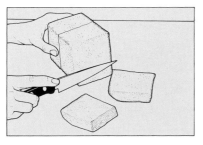

1 *Trim the cakes neatly and stick together at long sides with icing.*

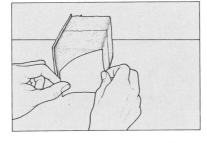

2 *Measure and cut pieces of rice paper to fit sides and top of cooker. Spread cake with icing and stick paper all over.*

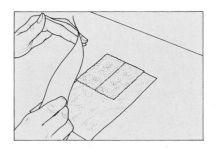

3 *Cut two pieces of rice paper to fit back and to extend above to form instrument panel of cooker. Sandwich two wafers between these with icing.*

6 *Stick 'hotplates' onto cooker. Make saucepans from mini rolls and Matchmakers and add suitable contents.*

4 *When dry stick on chocolate drops for knobs and decorate with red gel. Stick to back of cooker with icing.*

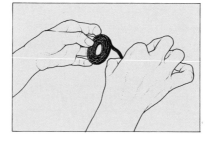

5 *Take out centres of liquorice whirls. Undo and cut off some of the outside to make smaller.*

CHRISTMAS PUDDING

2 chocolate cake mixes baked in basin
1 packet plain chocolate cake covering
plain chocolate chips
1 packet white chocolate cake covering
icing holly / Matchmakers

This is one of my favourites – it's very simple but looks immediately Christmassy and festive. Also, as some people don't like icing, it's good to use melted chocolate for a change. If you can't get hold of the white cake covering then bars of white chocolate work almost as well.

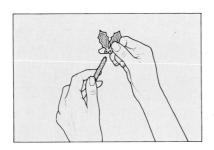

1 *When cake is completely cool cover with melted chocolate cake covering. Leave a few minutes until tacky.*

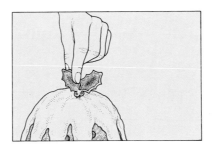

2 *Press chocolate chips all around cake. Lift carefully onto a plate and put into fridge to get completely cool and hard.*

3 *Melt white chocolate. Allow it to cool a little (or it will melt the pudding) but still remain runny, then pour onto top of cake, letting it run down sides to look like cream.*

6 *Put the pudding on a suitable plate.*

4 *Stick holly to pieces of Matchmaker with a little chocolate. Leave to set.*

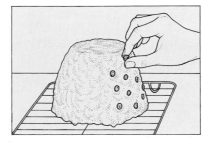

5 *Stick the holly into top of pudding.*

SAILING BOAT

I'd hardly call this a streamlined yacht, but it does have a sort of chunky charm, and boats are always popular.

1 deep sponge cake (2 packets sponge mix baked in loaf tin)
1 tube ready-to-use chocolate icing
large sheet rice paper / 2 long Matchmakers
1 tube ready-to-use blue icing
1 tube ready-to-use white icing
food colouring

1 *Trim front and back of cake to boat shape.*

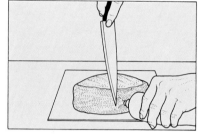

2 *Cover sides with chocolate icing and smooth with wet knife.*

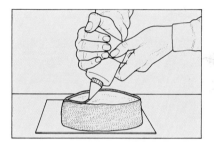

3 *Smooth white icing over deck. Pipe edging with chocolate.*

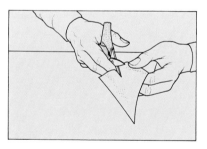

4 *Cut sails from rice paper.*

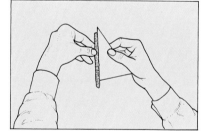

5 *Stick sails to mast with icing, letting mast extend at bottom.*

6 *Push sail into deck. Put boat on cake board and ice board blue. Pipe name on boat and pipe spray onto sea. Make flag from piece of Matchmaker and coloured rice paper.*

CANDLES

You could dress these up with a little edible holly for the Christmas table, or left plain they would be lovely at a confirmation or other church occasion.

1 plain Swiss roll
½ lb/250 g fondant
jam
Matchmakers
red colouring
yellow colouring

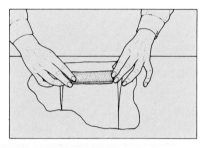

1 *Roll out fondant slightly longer than Swiss roll. Brush with jam and roll up cake in it, tucking one end under.*

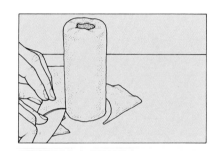

2 *Brush uncovered end with jam, stand on fondant and cut away excess to cover top. Turn right side up.*

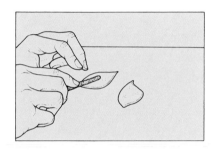

3 *Cut two pieces of fondant to flame shape. Wet and sandwich together, placing Matchmaker between. Let dry.*

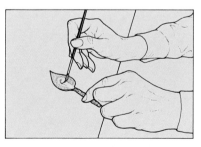

4 *Paint flame with yellow and red. Push into candle.*

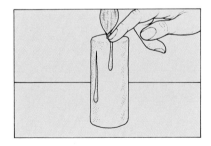

5 *Roll little pieces of fondant with blobs on the ends and stick to candle with a little water.*

6 *Make more drips around top of candle to cover join. Make smaller candles as required by using mini rolls.*

80

DINOSAURS

1 large rectangular sponge cake (3 mixes in baking tray)
1 packet rock cake mix / light and dark soft brown sugar
8 chocolate finger biscuits / 3 chocolate mini rolls
chocolate cake covering / thin chocolate crisp mints
2 chocolates / 1 tube ready-to-use white icing / edible red gel
chocolate decorations / silver balls
1 tube ready-to-use blue icing / angelica

What is the fascination of dinosaurs? There's no doubt that they intrigue boys and girls today as much as they ever did and although these are not strictly accurate they have enough of a dinosaurish feel to make a child very happy.

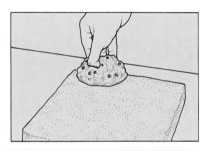

1 Bake rock cake mix in rough piles. Stick to rear of sponge with icing (any colour).

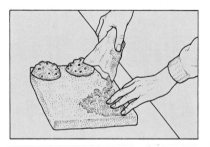

2 Spread entire cake with icing (any colour) and sprinkle with light and dark sugar. Press in with fingers.

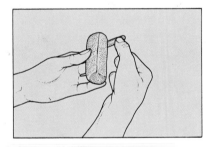

3 To make dinosaurs' legs, necks and tails, stick chocolate biscuits to mini rolls with melted cake covering, holding for a few seconds until set.

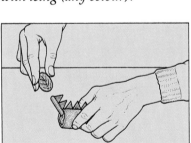

4 For the fierce one cut mint crisps into triangles and stick along back. Stick a chocolate for head and pipe white teeth tipped with red gel.

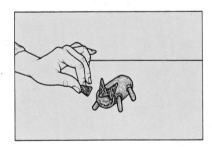

5 Use chocolate decorations for frill around triceratops' neck, sticking them before you add the head.

6 Brontosaurus has broken biscuit for the head. Add silver ball eyes to all of them. Pipe white bones and add red gel blood. Pipe a blue pool and stick angelica grass around it. Carefully place dinosaurs onto cake.

SPIDER

1 sponge sandwich
1 tube ready-to-use chocolate icing
1 tube ready-to-use white icing
1 liquorice whirl
1 rum truffle cake
2 chocolate drops

I know some people hate spiders but I've always had rather a soft spot for them. The creature made of chocolate icing in the corner of the window is meant to be a fly, but the way I've piped him he looks more like another type of spider.

1 *Spread cake with white icing.*

2 *Pipe web with chocolate icing.*

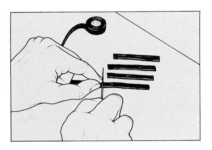

3 *Unravel liquorice and cut strips for legs.*

6 *Cut web shape around edge of cake with sharp knife. Put spider on top.*

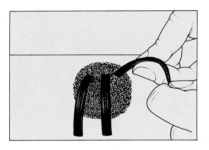

4 *Make slits with a knife in truffle and push in legs.*

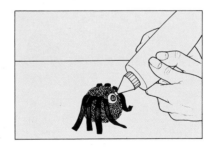

5 *Pipe white eyes and add chocolate drop pupils.*

TABLE

It's very satisfying to use fondant icing to look like material – if you work quickly it can drape beautifully. There's something slightly surreal about this table – I wonder who is going to sit at it?

1 rectangular sponge (1 packet sponge baked in loaf tin)
½ lb/250 g white fondant
5 chocolate mini rolls / sugar flowers,
green decorating gel
white icing or jam / angelica / chocolate cup / marzipan fruit

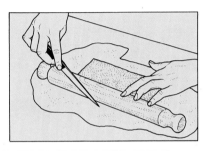

1 *Roll out fondant and cut a rectangle large enough to cover table top and half way down legs.*

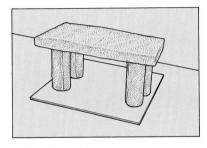

2 *Trim mini rolls and stick to corners of table.*

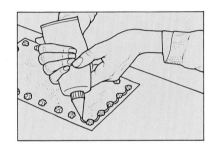

3 *Working as fast as possible decorate cloth with sugar flowers and gel.*

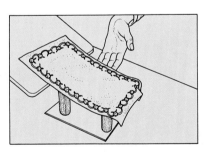

4 *Spread table with icing or jam and quickly drape cloth over it.*

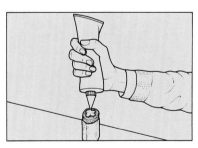

5 *Cover two thirds of remaining mini roll with fondant and then spread bare portion with icing.*

6 *Press flowers into icing. Cut angelica leaves and stick between flowers. Fill chocolate cup with fruit. Put both on table.*

CROWN

two 6 in/15 cm round fruit cakes / jam
3 packets yellow marzipan
1 tube ready-to-use red icing
1 tube ready-to-use white icing
clear and coloured boiled sweets / silver balls
black food colouring

Why not make the man in your life feel like a king on his birthday? Or it would do just as well for a queen. If it was for a party and you need a larger cake then you could make a cushion out of sponge covered with red fondant.

1 *Stick the two cakes together with jam and a circle of marzipan. Trim top to a rounded shape.*

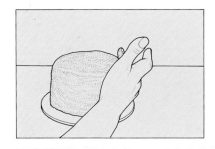

2 *Roll out marzipan and cover cake. Spread with red icing then smooth with wet fingers.*

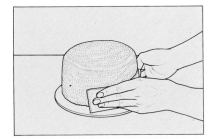

3 *Roll and cut a strip of marzipan about half the depth of the cake. Wrap this around the bottom of the cake.*

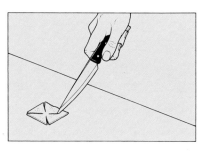

4 *Roll a strip of marzipan and cut squares. Cut slashes to corners to make shapes as shown.*

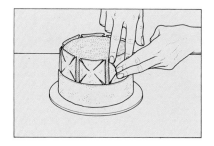

5 *Stick shapes onto top of strip.*

6 *With shell nozzle pipe ermine around base, with small nozzle pipe pearls. Stick on sweets and silver balls. Paint black flecks onto ermine.*

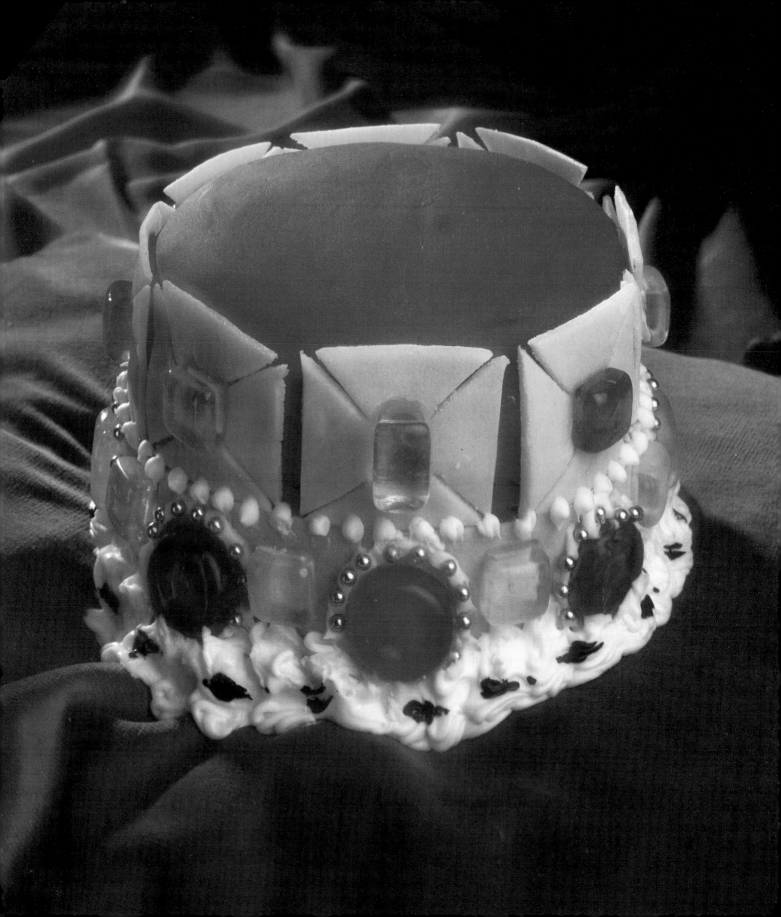

BASIC RECIPES

FONDANT ICING

1lb/500g icing sugar / 1 egg white
1 tablespoon liquid glucose

Sieve icing sugar into a bowl and mix in the egg white and glucose with a spoon. Knead with the fingers until smooth and pliable. Keep in a plastic bag when not in use.

You can replace the ready-to-use tubes of icing used in the recipes with either of the following:

BUTTER ICING

4 oz/100 g butter / 8oz/250g sieved icing sugar
2 teaspoons lemon juice

Beat the butter in a bowl with a wooden spoon until light and fluffy then beat in the icing sugar and lemon juice.

ROYAL ICING

1lb/500g sieved icing sugar
2 egg whites / 2 teaspoons lemon juice

Break the egg whites with a fork then add with the lemon juice to the icing sugar in a bowl little by little, beating well until you achieve the desired consistency.

MERINGUE

4oz/120g castor sugar / 2 egg whites

Make sure the sugar and egg whites are at room temperature. Prepare a baking sheet by lining with foil or greaseproof paper. For a large meringue mark out the circle and then brush the lining with oil. Whisk the egg whites until they are very stiff and stand in peaks. Sift half the sugar onto the whites and beat in lightly. The mixture should look smooth and glossy. Sift in the rest of the sugar in two or three stages and fold in lightly with a large metal spoon.

Pour the meringue onto the baking sheet and spread to shape with a metal spatula. It should be about ¾ in / 2 cm in depth. If you prefer the meringue can be piped in a circle starting from the centre. For small meringues use two spoons and lay spoonfuls on the sheet, or pipe small whirls.

Preheat the oven to 140°C, 275°F, gas 1 and bake for 1½ to 2½ hours according to size. The oven may be switched off and the meringue left in longer. It must dry out and turn a pale creamy colour. This quantity will make one 8in / 20cm meringue or 12 small ones.